# OSI

## Reference Model

**Somayeh Babaei Tarkami**

**Ali Mohammadiounotikandi**

**Copyrights © 2022**

**All Rights Reserved for the Authors**

*No part of this book may be reprinted or reproduced and utilized in any electronic, mechanical, or other means now known or hereafter invented, including photocopying and recording or any information storage or retrieval system, without permission in writing from the authors. Moreover, the author keeps all the publication rights of this book for themselves.*

**Title**: OSI Reference Model

**Author**: Somayeh Babaei Tarkami, Ali Mohammadiounotikandi

**Cover Designer**: Somayeh Babaei Tarkami

**Publisher**: American Academic Research, USA

**ISBN**: 9781947464391

# Contents

About the authors .................................................................. 4
Introduction ............................................................................ 7
OSI Reference Model .............................................................. 9
Transmission Medium Modes ............................................. 19
Simplex mode ........................................................................ 19
Functions of Data Link Layer ............................................... 23
Framing .................................................................................. 23
Network .................................................................................. 25
Presentation ........................................................................... 40
Application ............................................................................ 46
OSI Model in Action ............................................................. 53
Advantages of OSI Model .................................................... 61
OSI vs. TCP/IP Model .......................................................... 62
Other important differences: .............................................. 63
References .............................................................................. 64

# About the authors

**Somayeh Babaei Tarkami** is an Iranian-Turkish author and graphic designer, born in 1983 in Iran. With a passion for art and design from a young age, Somayeh pursued a career in graphic design and obtained a Master's degree in the field. She has over 15 years of experience in advertising and sales management, as well as more than 8 years of research activity in the IT industry and information security management.

Somayeh is also an IT security consultant, with certifications in ISO and PMP, demonstrating her commitment to staying up-to-date with the latest developments in the field. As the founder of Bahman Information Processing Company, she holds DBA certificates, ISO 9001, and ISO 27001.

In addition to her work in design and security, Somayeh is an accomplished writer with several published works exploring topics such as design, creativity, and entrepreneurship. Her writing draws on her own experiences as a designer and consultant, offering insights and advice to aspiring creatives and entrepreneurs.

Somayeh is an active member of the creative community in Iran and beyond, participating in exhibitions, conferences, and workshops to share her knowledge and expertise. Her work has earned her a reputation as a leading voice in the fields of design and security, and she continues to inspire others with her creativity and insight.

**Ali Mohammadioun Otikandi** is an Iranian-Turkish author and IT professional born in 1986 in Iran. Growing up in Iran, Ali developed an interest in literature and technology at an early age, leading him to pursue a career in the IT field while also exploring his passion for writing.

After completing his education in computer science and obtaining a Master's degree in IT, Ali began working in the IT industry, gaining expertise in areas such as software development, network engineering, and information security. He has earned several professional certifications, including CompTIA, Microsoft, Linux, ISACA, and ISO 27001 and 9001, demonstrating his commitment to staying up-to-date with the latest developments in the field.

He has also authored several articles in respected academic journals, earning recognition from the ISI and Scopus indices.

The title "Security Reference in Computer Networks Based on the Topics of Security+" has been selected as one of the references for the Ph.D. entrance exam of Information Technology Engineering, 2022, Iran.

The title "Network+ from 0 to 100" has been chosen as the selected book of the Agriculture Bank for teaching and research purposes, 2022, Iran.

Achieved the first stage of the National Students Mathematics Olympiad, 2002, Iran.

Several books and ideas have been published in the United States before that.

# Introduction

Welcome to our book on the OSI model! In this book, we will explore the Open Systems Interconnection (OSI) model, which is a conceptual framework for network communication. The OSI model provides a standard for communication between different systems by breaking down the communication process into seven layers.

As two authors with experience in networking, we have come to appreciate the importance of the OSI model in understanding how networks operate. This book is intended for anyone interested in networking, from students learning about networking for the first time to professionals who need a refresher on the OSI model.

In this book, we will explore each layer of the OSI model in detail, discussing its purpose and the protocols that operate at that layer. We will also examine how the layers interact with each other to facilitate communication between devices on a network.

We will start by discussing the physical layer, which deals with the physical aspects of transmitting data across a network, such as the cables, connectors, and other hardware used in network communication. We will then move on to the data link layer, which is responsible for transmitting data between two directly connected devices.

From there, we will explore the network layer, which is responsible for routing data between networks. We will then discuss the transport layer, which provides end-to-end communication between devices. The session layer is responsible for establishing, maintaining, and terminating sessions between devices. The presentation layer is responsible for converting data into a format that can be understood by the application layer. Finally, we will discuss the application layer, which provides services to applications running on a network.

By the end of this book, readers will have a comprehensive understanding of the OSI model and how it operates to enable communication between devices on a network. We hope that this book will serve as a valuable resource for anyone interested in networking and will help readers develop the skills they need to build and maintain networks effectively.

# OSI Reference Model

Initially, network development was chaotic. Each vendor provided their specialized solution. The disadvantage was that one vendor's solution did not work with the solution of another vendor. This is the origin of the OSI model. With a layered network, our hardware vendors would design network hardware, while others would create software for the application layer. We can build networks that are interoperable if we use an open model that everyone agrees on.

To address this issue, the International Organization for Standardization (ISO) investigated various network models, resulting in the 1984 release of the OSI model. Most vendors now build networks using the OSI model, and hardware from different vendors is interchangeable.

The OSI model is not only a network compatibility model; it is also one of the BEST methods for teaching people about networks.

Remember this because the OSI model will come up frequently when studying networking.

# The OSI model looks like this

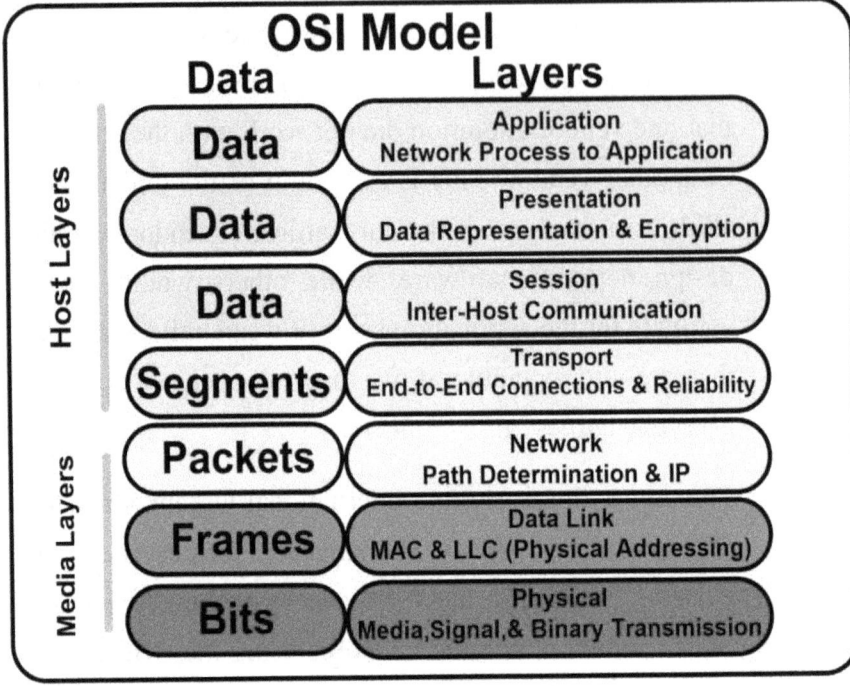

The OSI model has seven layers, and we're starting at the bottom and working our way up. To begin, consider the physical layer

## Physical Layer

The Physical Layer is the OSI Model's lowest layer, and it is a physical and electrical representation of the system. It consists of various network components such as power plugs, connectors, receivers, and cable types. The Physical Layer is responsible for transporting data bits from one device (such as a computer) to another (s). The Physical Layer defines the encoding types (how the 0's and 1's in a signal are encoded). The Physical Layer is responsible for transmitting unstructured raw data streams over a physical medium.

## Functions Performed

The physical Layer is the lowest layer in the Open System Interconnection (OSI) Model, and it is a physical and electrical representation of the system. It is made up of various network components such as power plugs, connectors, receivers, and cable types, among others. The physical layer transfers data bits from one device (such as a computer) to another. The physical layer defines the types of encoding (how the 0's and 1's in a signal are encoded). The physical Layer is in charge of communicating unstructured raw data streams over a physical medium.

The Physical Layer of the OSI Model performs the following fundamental functions:

- The Physical Layer keeps the data rate constant (how many bits a sender can send per second).
- It performs bit synchronization.
- It aids in the selection of Transmission Medium (direction of data transfer).

- It aids in the selection of Physical Topology (Mesh, Star, Bus, Ring) (Topology through which we can connect the devices.

- It aids in the determination of Physical Medium and Interface decisions.

- It has two configuration options: point configuration and multi-point configuration.

- It serves as a bridge between devices (such as PCs or computers) and the transmission medium.

- It has a protocol data unit that is measured in bits.

- In this layer, devices such as hubs, Ethernet, and so on are used.

- This layer is classified as a Hardware Layer (since the hardware layer is responsible for all the physical connection establishment and processing too).

- It includes a crucial feature known as modulation, which is the process of converting data into radio waves by adding information to an electrical or optical nerve signal.

- It also includes a switching mechanism for forwarding data packets from one port (sender port) to the leading destination port.

## Physical Topologies

Physical topology or network topology refers to the geographic representation of linking devices. The following are the four types of physical topology:

### Mesh Topology

Every device in a mesh topology should have a dedicated point-to-point connection with every other device in the network. Because the two devices are connected via a dedicated point-to-point connection, data is more secure. Mesh Topology is more difficult to set up due to its complexity.

### Star Topology

The device in a star topology should have a dedicated point-to-point connection with a central controller or hub. In comparison to Mesh Topology, Star Topology is simpler to install and reconnect. The fault Tolerance Technique does not exist in Star Topology.

### Bus Topology

Bus topology is a network topology in which all devices or nodes are linked to a single communication line known as a bus. All devices in a bus topology share the same communication channel, which means that data transmitted by one device is accessible to all other devices on the network.

Because there is no central device or hub, the bus topology is simple and inexpensive to implement.

It is frequently used in small networks, such as those found in homes, small businesses, and classrooms. One advantage of bus topology is the ease with which devices can be added or removed from the network without interfering with the operation of the other devices. However, if the main communication line fails or is damaged, the entire network may be affected. Furthermore, because all devices share the same communication channel, the network can become congested if multiple devices attempt to transmit data at the same time.

Overall, bus topology is a simple and cost-effective solution for small networks with low traffic volume. However, it may not be suitable for larger

networks or those with high traffic demands, were other topologies, such as

star or mesh may be more appropriate.

## Ring Topology

Ring topology is a computer network topology in which nodes are connected in a circular pattern. In this topology, each node is connected to two neighboring nodes, and data is transmitted unidirectionally around the ring.

The ring topology has both benefits and drawbacks. Because there is no single point of failure, the network can handle high traffic loads and provide a reliable connection. Furthermore, by adding new nodes to the ring, the network can be easily expanded.

However, one disadvantage of the ring topology is that a single node failure can bring the entire network down.

Furthermore, when there is a lot of traffic, the network can become slow because data has to travel around the entire ring before it gets to its destination. Furthermore, troubleshooting the network can be challenging because any node failure can affect the entire ring.

In-ring topologies, token-based data transmission is used. This means that a token is passed around the ring, and only the node that has the token can transmit data. When a node needs to send data, it takes possession of the token, sends the data, and then releases it. This prevents network collisions by allowing only one node to transmit data at a time.

Ring topology is used in a variety of applications, including telecommunications networks, local area networks (LANs), and metropolitan area networks

(MANs). A networking technology that can be implemented in a ring topology is Ethernet.

## Point to Point configuration

A point-to-point (PTP) network topology is one in which two nodes are directly connected via a dedicated communication channel. This configuration is also known as a "dedicated link" because the communication channel is only used by the two nodes.

There is no intermediate device, such as a switch or router, between the two nodes in a point-to-point configuration. A physical communication channel, such as a copper or fiber optic cable, or a wireless communication channel, such as a microwave or satellite link, can be used.

High speed, low latency, and high security are all advantages of point-to-point configuration. There is no interference from other nodes or devices on the network because the communication channel is dedicated to the two nodes. This eliminates the need for network addressing or routing, which simplifies network management.

In WAN (Wide Area Network) connections between two remote locations, such as a headquarters and a branch office, point-to-point configurations are commonly used. They are also used in telecommunication networks, where fast and reliable connections are required for voice and data transmission.

Point-to-point connections have the disadvantage of being expensive to set up and maintain, especially for long-distance connections. They also lack the scalability of other network topologies like mesh or ring. Furthermore, if the communication channel fails, the two nodes will lose connectivity, necessitating redundancy, and failover planning.

## Multi-Point configuration

A Multi-Point configuration in networking refers to a network topology in which three or more devices are connected to the same communication channel, allowing all devices to communicate with each other at the same time.

A Multi-Point configuration is commonly used in LANs and WANs and can be implemented using a variety of networking technologies such as Ethernet, Wi-Fi, and Bluetooth.

A Wi-Fi network is a common example of a Multi-Point configuration, in which multiple devices, such as smartphones, laptops, and smart home devices, are connected to the same wireless access point, allowing them to communicate and access the internet.

A bus topology is another example, in which all devices are connected to a central cable or backbone, allowing them to communicate with one another. This network topology was widely used in early Ethernet networks.

Multi-point configurations are also common in video conferencing systems, where multiple participants can join the same conference call and communicate in real-time.

Overall, Multi-Point configurations are useful for enabling communication and collaboration among multiple devices and users, making them an essential component of modern networking.

# Transmission Medium Modes

**Simplex mode**

In this mode, only one of two devices can transmit data, while the other can only receive data. Input from keyboards, monitors, TV broadcasting, radio broadcasting, and so on.

**Half Duplex mode**

In this mode, both devices can send and receive data but only one at a time and not simultaneously. For example, a walkie-talkie, a railway track, and so on.

**Full-Duplex mode**

In this mode, both devices can send and receive data at the same time. Telephone systems, chat applications, and so on are examples.

## Point to Point configuration

A point-to-point configuration in networking refers to a network topology in which two devices are connected directly to each other, with no intermediate devices or connections between them. This type of configuration is also known as a "dedicated link" or "point-to-point link."

Point-to-point networks can be built with a variety of physical connections, including copper wires, fiber optic cables, and wireless transmissions. Serial connections between two routers or switches leased lines between two locations, and direct wireless links between two devices are all examples of point-to-point connections.

One of the primary benefits of point-to-point configurations is their ease of use and dependability. There is less chance of network congestion, interference, or failure because there are no intermediate devices or connections. Point-to-point links also have low latency, which is advantageous for applications requiring quick and responsive communication, such as video conferencing or online gaming.

Another benefit of point-to-point configurations is security. Because the connection is limited to two devices, there is less risk of unauthorized access or data interception.

However, point-to-point networks have some limitations. They are usually more expensive to set up and maintain than other types of topologies, and they may not scale well for large networks with a large number of devices.

Furthermore, because point-to-point networks are limited to two devices, they may not be appropriate for applications requiring communication between multiple devices.

Overall, point-to-point networking configurations are a useful tool, especially for applications that require high reliability, low latency, and security. They are not, however, a one-size-fits-all solution, and their advantages and disadvantages should be carefully considered before implementation.

## Data Link

The data link layer is the most reliable node-to-node data delivery layer. It constructs frames from network layer packets and sends them to the physical layer. It also synchronizes the data that will be sent over the network. Error control is straightforward. After that, the encoded data is sent to the physical.

Error detection bits are used in the data link layer. It also corrects errors. Incoming messages are used to create frames. Following transmission, the system waits for acknowledgments. Messages can be sent with confidence.

The data link layer's primary function is to transform a raw transmission facility into a line that appears to the network layer to be free of undetected transmission errors. It accomplishes this task by requiring the sender to divide the input data into data frames (typically a few hundred or thousand bytes) and transmit the frames sequentially. The receiver acknowledges receipt of each frame by sending back an acknowledgment frame if the service is reliable.

# Functions of Data Link Layer

## Framing

Frames are streams of network layer bits that are converted into manageable data units. The Data Link Layer is in charge of splitting the bit stream.

## Physical Location

If the frames are to be distributed to different systems on the network, the Data Link layer adds a header to the frame to define the sender's or receiver's physical address.

## Flow Management

Flow control prevents a fast transmitter from sending data to a slow receiver by buffering the extra bit. This prevents traffic congestion on the receiving end.

## Controlling Errors

To control errors, a trailer at the end of the frame is used. This mechanism also avoids frame duplication. A mechanism to prevent frame duplication is included in Data Link Layers.

## Access Control

When two or more devices are connected to the same link, the protocols of this layer determine which device controls the link at any given time.

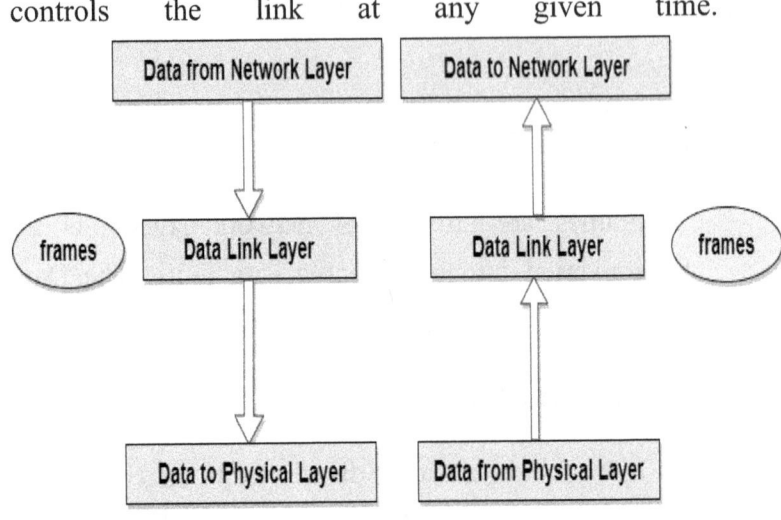

## Problems with Data Link Layer Design

The issue in the data link layer (and most higher layers) is keeping a fast transmitter from drowning a slow receiver in data. A traffic control mechanism is frequently required to inform the transmitter of the receiver's current buffer space. Flow control and error handling are frequently used in tandem.

Broadcast networks face an additional challenge at the data link layer: controlling access to the shared channel. This problem is handled by the data link layer's Medium Access Control (MAC) sublayer.

# Network

Network-to-network connections enable the Internet to function. The Internet communications process's "network layer" is where these connections are made by sending data packets back and forth between different networks. Layer 3 of the seven-layer OSI model is the network layer (shown below). One of the primary protocols used at this layer is the Internet Protocol (IP), along with several other protocols for routing, testing, and encryption.

Assume Bob and Alice are both connected to the same LAN and Bob wants to send a message to Alice. Because Bob and Alice are both on the same network, he could send it to her computer directly over the network. If Alice is on a different LAN that is several miles away, Bob's message must be addressed and sent to Alice's network before it can reach her computer, which is a network layer process.

A network is a collection of two or more computing devices that are linked together. All network devices are typically connected to a central hub, such as a router. A network can also have subnetworks or smaller subdivisions of the network.

Subnetting is a technique for managing thousands of IP addresses and connected devices on very large networks, such as those provided by ISPs.

Consider the Internet to be a network of networks: computers are connected within networks that connect to other networks. This enables these computers to communicate with other computers, both near and far.

## Network

Everything that has to do with inter-network connections happens at the network layer. Configuring data packet routes, determining whether a server in another network is operational, and addressing and receiving IP packets from other networks are all examples of this. Because the vast majority of Internet traffic is transmitted via IP, this final process is perhaps the most critical.

## Packet

All data transmitted over the Internet is broken down into smaller chunks known as "packets." When Bob sends a message to Alice, for example, it is disassembled and reassembled on Alice's computer.

A packet is composed of two parts: the header, which contains information about the packet, and the body, which contains the data to be transmitted.

When a packet is sent over the Internet, networking software at the network layer attaches a header to it, which networking software on the receiving end can use to determine how to handle the packet.

The header of each packet contains information about its content, source, and destination (somewhat like stamping an envelope with a destination and return address). An IP header, for example, contains each packet's destination IP address, total size, whether or not the packet was fragmented in transit, and a count of how many networks the packet has passed through.

## OSI model

The OSI model (Open Systems Interconnection model) is a conceptual model that specifies how data should be communicated between computer systems. It was created in the 1980s by the International Organization for Standardization (ISO).

The OSI model is divided into seven layers, each of which has its own set of functions and protocols. These layers are listed in order from bottom to top:

This layer is concerned with the physical transmission of data over a medium. It specifies the transmission medium's electrical, mechanical, and physical properties.

Data link layer: This layer is in charge of ensuring that data is reliably transmitted between two nodes on the same network. It divides data into frames and detects and corrects errors.

The network layer is in charge of routing data between different networks. It can handle congestion control and determines the best path for data transmission.

This layer ensures the reliable end-to-end delivery of data between two applications. It can detect and correct errors, as well as control flow and congestion.

The session layer creates and manages connections between applications. It can also provide authentication and encryption services.

The presentation layer is in charge of representing data in a way that is meaningful to the application. It is capable of performing data compression and encryption.

The application layer serves as the interface between the user and the network. HTTP, FTP, and SMTP are among the protocols included.

Because it provides a common language for describing network communication, the OSI model is useful. It also enables the comparison and evaluation of various protocols and technologies based on their adherence to the model.

## OSI model vs. TCP/IP model

The TCP/IP model represents a new way of thinking about how the Internet operates. It divides the processes into four rather than seven layers. Some argue that the TCP/IP model better represents how the Internet works today, but the OSI model is still widely used to understand the Internet, and both models have benefits and drawbacks.

The TCP/IP model has four layers, which are as follows:

## Application layer

This corresponds roughly to layer 7 in the OSI model.

The transport layer is represented by Layer 4 in the OSI model.

The Internet layer is represented by Layer 3 of the OSI model.

The network access layer combines OSI layers 1 and 2 processes.

But where are OSI layers 5 and 6 in the TCP/IP model? According to some sources, the processes at OSI layers 5 and 6 are either no longer required in the modern Internet or belong to layers 7 and 4 (represented by TCP/IP layers 4 and 3).

Because the TCP protocol opens and maintains sessions at OSI layer 4, one could argue that OSI layer 5 (the "session" layer) is superfluous and is not represented in the TCP/IP model. Furthermore, rather than being presentation layer (OSI layer 6) processes, HTTPS encryption, and decryption are application layer (OSI layer 7 or TCP/IP layer 4) processes.

## At the network layer, protocols are used.

A protocol is a data format that is agreed upon that allows two or more devices to communicate and understand each other. A variety of protocols enable connections, testing, routing, and encryption at the network layer, including:

- IP
- IPsec
- ICMP
- IGMP
- GRE

# Transport Layer

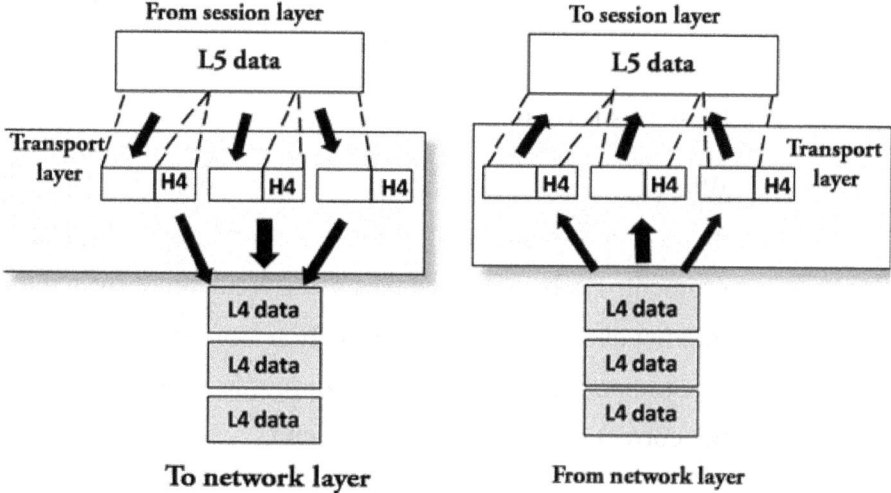

The Layer 4 Transport layer ensures that messages are sent in the correct order and that no data is duplicated.

The primary responsibility of the transport layer is to complete the data transfer.

It receives data from the upper layer and breaks it down into smaller units known as segments.

This layer is referred to as an end-to-end layer because it establishes a point-to-point connection between the source and destination to reliably deliver data.

This layer employs two protocols:

### Transmission Control Protocol

It is a standard protocol that allows systems to communicate over the internet.

It establishes and maintains host connections.

When data is transmitted over a TCP connection, it is divided into smaller units known as segments by the TCP protocol. Each segment takes a different route over the internet and arrives at the destination in a different order. The transmission control protocol reorders the packets in the correct order at the receiving end.

## User Datagram Protocol

The User Datagram Protocol is a transport layer protocol.

It is an untrustworthy transport protocol because when a packet is received, the receiver does not send any acknowledgment and the sender does not wait for any acknowledgment. As a result, a protocol loses its credibility.

Transport Layer Functions: Service-point Addressing: Data is transmitted from source to destination not only from one computer to another but also from one process to another because computers run multiple programs at the same time. The header, which contains the service-point address or port address, is added by the transport layer. The network layer is responsible for sending data from one computer to another, while the transport layer is responsible for routing the message to the appropriate process.

When the transport layer receives a message from the upper layer, it divides it into multiple segments, and each segment is assigned a unique sequence number. The transport layer reassembles the message using the sequence numbers when it arrives at its destination

## Connection administration

The transport layer performs two functions. Services are classified into two types: connection-oriented and connectionless. Each segment is treated as a separate packet by a connectionless service, and they all take different paths to their destination. A connection-oriented service connects to the transport layer at the destination machine before delivering packets. All packets in a connection-oriented service follow the same path. The transport layer also handles flow control, but it does so end-to-end rather than across a single link.

Error control: The transport layer is also in charge of error control. Instead of a single link, end-to-end error control is used. The sender transport layer ensures that messages arrive at their destination in perfect condition.

## Session

The Session Layer is the fifth layer in the Open System Interconnection (OSI) model. This layer enables users on different machines to have active communication sessions. It is in charge of creating, maintaining, synchronizing, and terminating end-user application sessions.

Streams of data are received and marked in the Session Layer before being properly resynchronized, preventing message ends from being cut initially and preventing further data loss. This layer is in charge of linking the session entities. This layer receives and processes data from both the Session Layer and the Presentation Layer.

- Application Layer
- Presentation Layer
- Present Layer=> Session Layer
- Transport Layer
- Network Layer
- Data Layer
- Physical Layer

## Session Layer Operation

The Session Layer, the fifth layer in the OSI model, uses the Transport Layer's services to allow applications to establish, maintain, and synchronize sessions.

To establish a session connection, several steps must now be taken.

The first step is to correspond the session address with the shipping address. The second step is to determine the transport quality of service parameters that are required. The next step is to handle the negotiations that must occur between session parameters. Then we must send a limited amount of transparent user data. Finally, we must keep a close eye on the Data Transfer phase. The ability to send larger amounts of data files is critical and required.

## Session Layer Functions

The session layer, the fifth layer in the OSI model, is responsible for some critical functions that are required for establishing and maintaining a safe and secure connection.

Data from the Session's Presentation Layer Layer => Transport Layer Details

The Session Layer is in charge of the following tasks:

The Session Layer is a dialog controller that allows systems to communicate in either half-duplex or full-duplex mode.

This layer also manages tokens, preventing two users from accessing or attempting the same critical operation at the same time.

This layer enables synchronization by allowing the addition of checkpoints, which serve as data stream synchronization points.

Session checkpoints and recovery are also handled by this layer.

This layer's primary function is to open, close, and manage sessions between end-user application processes.

Remote procedure calls are commonly used in application environments to implement Session Layer services (RPCs).

The Session Layer is also responsible for synchronizing data from multiple sources.

This layer also manages one or more connections for each end-user application and communicates with the Presentation and Transport layers directly.

The Session Layer specifies checkpointing, adjournment, restart, and termination procedures.

The Session Layer uses checkpoints to allow communication sessions to be resumed from the point where the communication failed.

The Session Layer is in charge of retrieving or receiving data information from the preceding layer (transport layer) and transmitting it to the layer following it (presentation layer)

## Protocols for Session Layers

The Session Layer implements protocols necessary for safe, secure, and accurate communication between two end-user applications.

The protocols listed below are provided or used by the Session Layer.

AppleTalk Data Stream Protocol (ADSP)

ADSP is an Apple Inc. protocol that includes several features that enable local area networks to be connected without any prior configuration. This protocol was first made public in 1985.

This protocol strictly followed the OSI protocol layering model. ADSP employs two protocols to help the system self-configure: AppleTalk Address Resolution Protocol (AARP) and Name Binding Protocol (NBP).

## Real-time Transport Control Protocol

RTCP is a protocol that provides out-of-band statistics and control information to RTP (Real-time Transport Protocol) sessions. The primary function of RTCP is to provide feedback on the quality of service (QoS) in media distribution by sending statistical data to participants in the streaming multimedia session regularly, such as transmitted octet and packet counts or packet loss.

Protocol for Point-to-Point Tunneling

PPTP is a protocol that enables the establishment of virtual private networks. PPTP uses a TCP control channel and a Generic Routing Encapsulation tunnel to encapsulate PPP (Point-to-Point Protocol) packets. This protocol offers comparable levels of security and remote access to standard VPN (Virtual Private Network) products.

## Password Authentication Protocol

Password Authentication Protocol (PAP) is a password-based authentication protocol used by Point-to-Point Protocol to validate users (PPP). Almost all network operating systems and remote servers support PAP. PAP authentication occurs during the initial link establishment and verifies the client's identity using a two-way handshake (the client sends data and the server responds with Authentication-ACK (Acknowledgement) after the client's data is completely verified).

## Remote Procedure Call Protocol

The Remote Procedure Call Protocol (RPCP) is a protocol that is used when a computer program instructs a procedure (or a subroutine) to execute in a different address space without explicitly coding the remote interaction details. This is a type of client-server interaction that is usually accomplished through the use of a request-response message-passing system.

## Direct Sockets Protocol

SDP is a network protocol that allows socket streams to run over Remote Direct Memory Access (RDMA) network fabrics.

The goal of SDP is to provide an RDMA-accelerated alternative to the TCP protocol. The primary goal is to complete a single task in a way that is invisible to the application.

# Presentation

The Presentation Layer is the sixth layer in the Open System Interconnection (OSI) model. Because it serves as a data translator for the network, this layer is also known as the Translation layer. This layer extracts and manipulates data from the Application Layer so that it can be transmitted over the network. The primary responsibility of this layer is to provide or define the data format and encryption. The presentation layer is also known as the Syntax layer because it is in charge of ensuring that the data it receives or transmits to other layers has proper syntax.

## Presentation Layer Functions

Application Layer Data => Presentation Layer Information => Session Layer Information

The presentation layer, the sixth layer in the OSI model, performs many functions, which are discussed further below.

The presentation layer formats and encrypts data for network transmission.

This layer ensures that data is transmitted in such a way that the receiver understands it and can use it efficiently and effectively.

This layer manages abstract data structures and allows for the definition or exchange of high-level data structures (for example, banking records).

This layer performs encryption at the transmitter and decryption at the receiver.

This layer compresses data to reduce the bandwidth required for data transmission (the primary goal of data compression is to reduce the number of bits which is to be transmitted).

This layer is in charge of interoperability because different computers use different encoding methods (the ability of computers to exchange and use information).

This layer is primarily concerned with the presentation of data.

The presentation layer compresses data (reduces the number of bits used during transmission), which increases data throughput.

This layer addresses string representation issues as well.

Furthermore, the presentation layer is responsible for integrating all formats into a standardized format for efficient and effective communication.

For communication between dissimilar systems, this layer encodes the message from the user-dependent format to the common format and vice versa.

This layer deals with the syntax and semantics of the messages, as well as ensuring that the messages that are to be presented to the upper and lower layers are standardized and accurate.

The presentation layer is also in charge of information translation, formatting, and delivery for processing or display.

This layer also handles serialization (the process of translating a data structure or an object into a format that can be stored or transmitted easily).

## The OSI model's Presentation Layer Characteristics

When communicating between two network devices, the presentation layer, the sixth layer in the OSI model, is critical.

The following features are provided by the presentation layer:

If two or more devices are communicating over an encrypted connection, this presentation layer is in charge of both adding encryption on the sender's end and decoding encryption on the receiver's end so that the application layer can be represented with unencrypted, readable data

**This layer formats and encrypts data before it is sent across a network, removing compatibility issues.**

The Transfer Syntax is also negotiated by this presentation layer.

This presentation layer is also in charge of compressing data received from the application layer before delivering it to the session layer (the 5th layer in the OSI model), which improves communication speed and efficiency by reducing the amount of data to be transferred

**The Presentation Layer**

The presentation layer in the OSI model acts as a translator, converting data sent by the transmitting node's application layer into an acceptable and compatible data format based on the applicable network protocol and architecture. When data arrives at the receiving computer, the presentation layer converts it into a format that the application layer can understand. In other words, this layer handles any issues that arise when transmitted data must be viewed in a format other than the original format. The presentation layer, as a functional part of the OSI mode, performs a variety of data conversion algorithms and character translation functions. This layer is primarily in charge of managing two network characteristics: protocol and architecture

## Protocols for the Presentation Layer

The presentation layer, the OSI model's sixth but most important layer, performs several functions to ensure that the data being transferred or received is accurate and clear to all devices in a closed network.

The Presentation Layer must use the protocols defined below for translations and other specified functions.

### Protocol for Apple Filing

The Apple Filing Protocol is a proprietary network protocol (communications protocol) that provides services to macOS. This is the network file control protocol that was created specifically for Mac-based platforms.

### Protocol for Lightweight Presentation

The Lightweight Presentation Protocol (LWPP) is a protocol for providing ISO presentation services on top of TCP/IP-based protocol stacks.

### NetWare Core Protocol (NCP)

NetWare Core Protocol is a network protocol that allows users to access network services such as a file, print, directory, clock synchronization, messaging, remote command execution, and others.

### Representation of Network Data

The OSI model's implementation of the presentation layer, Network Data Representation, provides or defines various primitive data types, constructed data types, and data representation types

**External Data Representation**

The industry standard for data description and encoding is External Data Representation (XDR). It has been used to transfer data between computer architectures and has been used to communicate data between very different machines. The process of converting from a local representation to XDR is known as encoding, whereas the process of converting from XDR to a local representation is known as decoding.

**SSL stands for Secure Socket Layer**

The Secure Socket Layer protocol secures data sent between a web browser and a server. SSL encrypts the connection between a web server and a browser, ensuring that all information exchanged between them is private and secure.

# Application

It is the topmost layer of the OSI Model. The Application Layer's primary responsibility is to provide services to the user. Aside from that, it enables a user to access, retrieve, and manage files on a remote computer, as well as serves as the foundation for email forwarding and storage.

How applications communicate with one another is defined by the Application Layer protocols. Examples include HTTP, FTP, DNS, and other protocols.

First, let's define a few key terms:

Stateless Protocols: These protocols do not keep any data. Cookies are used by them

They do not necessitate the server saving server or session data. Stateless protocols increase transparency, dependability, and scalability.

## Stateful Protocol

These protocols are used to save data. The receiver may keep the session state of previous requests. As a result, they anticipate the server saving the status and session data. FTP, TCP, and other protocols are examples.

### Protocol for Inter-Band Communication

In-band control is a network protocol feature that governs data control. HTTP, SMTP, and so on.

## Out-of-band Control

Out-of-band control is a feature of network protocols that allows for unrestricted data control. For example, FTP RTT (Round-Trip Time): the time it takes for a small packet to travel from client to server and back.

## HTTP

The port number for HTTP (Hypertext Transfer Protocol) is 80.

Transport Control Protocol (TCP) protocol without an in-band State Protocol

TCP is used to achieve reliability because UDP is unreliable.

### There are two kinds of HTTP

### HTTP Persistence (1.1)

After sending response 1 RTT to all referenced objects, the server closes the connection.

lowered overhead

enhanced performance

### HTTP Non-Persistence (1.0)

The server closes the connection after sending response 2RTT to all referenced objects.

Overhead has increased.

Inadequate Results

## FTP

FTP (File Transfer Protocol)

Ports 20 (Data) and 21 (Control)

Transport Control Protocol (TCP)

Protocol of State

## Out-of-band Protocol

Reliable

Synchronous

Control Connection

Persistent Data Connection

Non-Persistent

## SMTP and POP

Simple Mail Transfer Protocol and Post Office Protocol

25th port of entry

TCP stands for Transport Control Protocol (TCP)

Both protocols have no state.

Both are in-band protocols.

The POP3 protocol uses two distinct ports:

I Port 110 is the standard non-encrypted POP2 port. ii) Port 995: Required if we want to securely connect using POP3.

Asynchronous as well as synchronous

**DNS (Domain Name System)**

The DNS (Domain Name System) is a hierarchical and distributed naming system used to translate domain names (for example, www.example.com) into IP addresses used to locate servers on the internet. It was created in the early 1980s and has since become an essential component of the internet infrastructure.

When you type a domain name into your web browser, the DNS system converts it into an IP address that your computer can use to connect to the appropriate server. The DNS system functions as follows:

1. A web browser is used by a user to enter a domain name.
2. The browser sends a DNS query to a DNS resolver (usually provided by the user's Internet service provider).
3. The resolver checks its cache to see if it has a record of the requested domain name's IP address. If it does, the IP address is returned to the browser, and the process is complete.

4. If the resolver does not have an IP address record, it sends a query to a root DNS server.

5. In response, the root server provides the IP address of the appropriate top-level domain (TLD) server (e.g. .com, .org, .net, etc.).

6. The resolver then sends a query to the appropriate TLD server, which response with the IP address of the domain's authoritative name server.

7. The resolver then sends a query to the authoritative name server, which response with the requested domain's IP address.

8. The resolver saves the IP address and returns it to the browser.

The DNS system is critical to the internet's operation because it allows users to connect to websites and other internet services without having to remember numerical IP addresses. Because multiple IP addresses can be associated with a single domain name, it also allows for efficient load balancing and fault tolerance.

**Root Servers**

There are 13 root servers located all over the world.

They are further classified as follows:

.org

.com

.in

.mil

.edu

**There are several types of DOMAIN Generic Domains:**

.com (commercial)

.edu (educational)

and.mil (military) domain extensions (military)

In (India)

.us (United States)

.ca (Canada) are examples of country domains (Canada)

**Top Level Domains (TLDs):**

.com and.net there are two methods for resolving DNS queries:

Iterative Recursion

There are three levels of name servers: root, intermediate, and secondary.

A root name server is a name server for the Internet's Domain Name System's root zone (DNS)

The server of the highest caliber

It manages com, org, and edu, as well as all top-level country domains such as UK, ca, and in.

**Authenticated name servers**

This is the organization's DNS server, and it provides an authoritative hostname for IP mapping for the organization's servers.

# OSI Model in Action

All this talk about layers is nice, but where is the action? We can see the different layers of the OSI model in action if we capture network traffic on our computer.

Wireshark is a network capture tool that allows us to capture and examine all packets that our computer receives/transmits.

After downloading and installing Wireshark, navigate to the Capture menu and select "Options":

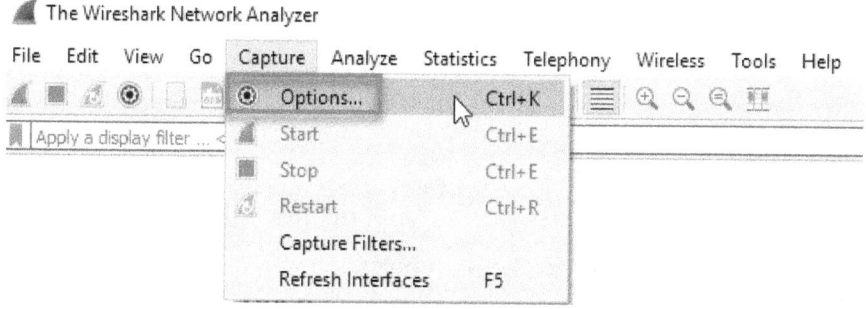

A list of all your network cards will now appear

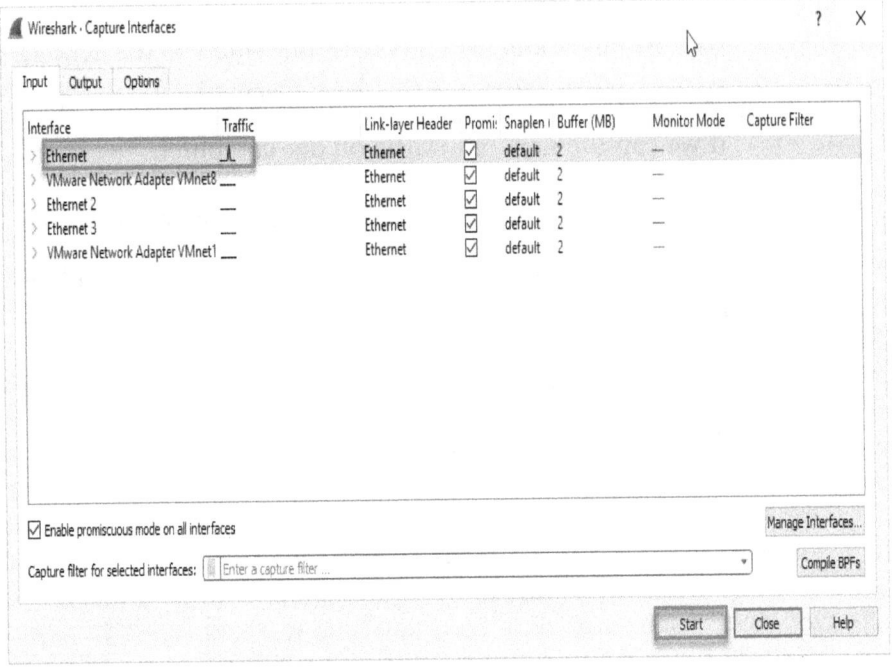

In my case, I'd like to capture the Ethernet interface. When you press the Start button, it will capture all packets entering and leaving the network.

The interface is being exited. It will look like this

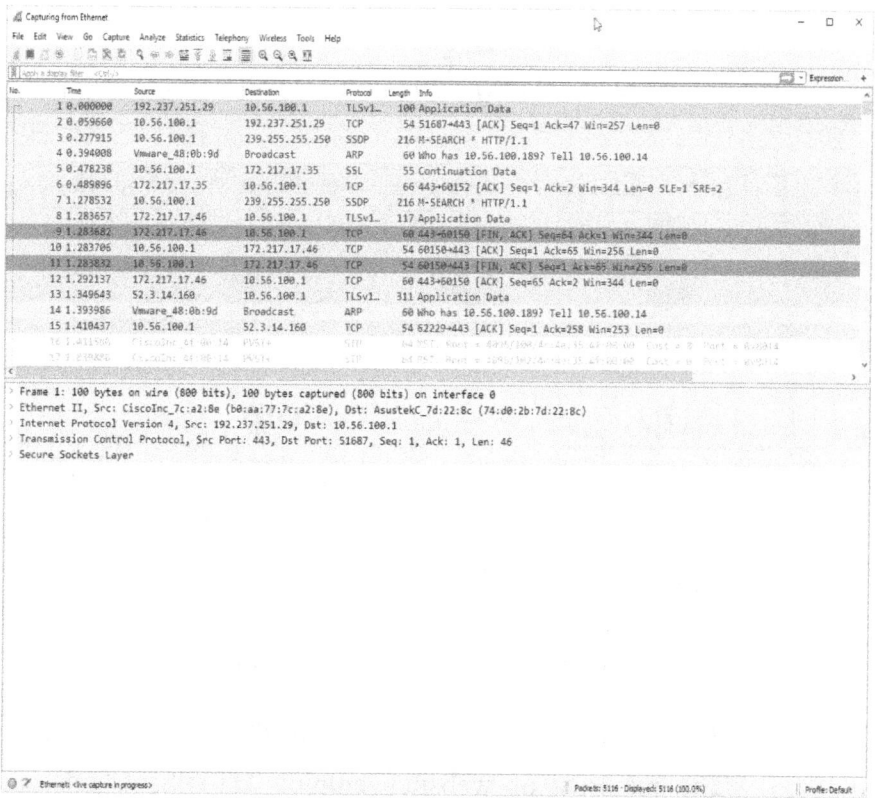

Don't be concerned about what you see here; there will be a lot of it. You will become more familiar with the various networking protocols and their packets/frames as you learn more about networking. We're going to take a single frame and look at it closely. To achieve this, we will use a filter to ensure that

Wireshark only displays the following traffic

 Capturing from Ethernet

File    Edit    View    Go    Capture

 http.host=="cisco.com"

In the green bar on the top left, enter the following filter:

HTTP.Host=="cisco.com"

Now, open your web browser and go to http://cisco.com.

Please enter http://cisco.com rather than just cisco.com. The majority of websites employ HTTPS, which is encrypted by default.

After the website has loaded, open Wireshark

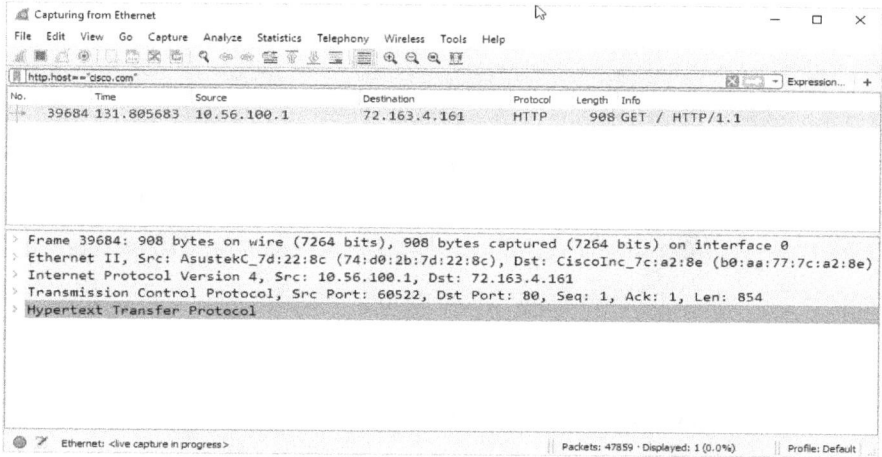

Our browser's request to access the Cisco.com website will arrive in a single packet. The contents of this frame can be seen in the bottom half of the screen. Let me explain in greater detail:

```
Frame 39684: 908 bytes on wire (7264 bits), 908 bytes captured (7264 bits) on interface 0
    Interface id: 0 (\Device\NPF_{D9C31349-9E36-46B2-B38A-24E2DF209E42})
    Encapsulation type: Ethernet (1)
    Arrival Time: Oct 26, 2016 15:37:24.127232000 W. Europe Summer Time
    [Time shift for this packet: 0.000000000 seconds]
    Epoch Time: 1477489044.127232000 seconds
    [Time delta from previous captured frame: 0.000106000 seconds]
    [Time delta from previous displayed frame: 0.000000000 seconds]
    [Time since reference or first frame: 131.805683000 seconds]
    Frame Number: 39684
    Frame Length: 908 bytes (7264 bits)
    Capture Length: 908 bytes (7264 bits)
    [Frame is marked: False]
    [Frame is ignored: False]
    [Protocols in frame: eth:ethertype:ip:tcp:http]
    [Coloring Rule Name: HTTP]
    [Coloring Rule String: http || tcp.port == 80 || http2]
```

The first bit of information has been added by Wireshark. It indicates that we have received a 908-byte Ethernet frame. It also shows the expected arrival time. The second section is as follows:

```
> Ethernet II, Src: AsustekC_7d:22:8c (74:d0:2b:7d:22:8c), Dst: CiscoInc_7c:a2:8e (b0:aa:77:7c:a2:8e)
   > Destination: CiscoInc_7c:a2:8e (b0:aa:77:7c:a2:8e)
   > Source: AsustekC_7d:22:8c (74:d0:2b:7d:22:8c)
     Type: IPv4 (0x0800)
```

The second layer of the OSI model is depicted above. The source and destination MAC addresses are displayed in the Ethernet frame. It also indicates the type of packet, in this case, an IPv4 packet in our Ethernet frame.

Let's take a look:

```
> Internet Protocol Version 4, Src: 10.56.100.1, Dst: 72.163.4.161
    0100 .... = Version: 4
    .... 0101 = Header Length: 20 bytes (5)
  > Differentiated Services Field: 0x00 (DSCP: CS0, ECN: Not-ECT)
    Total Length: 894
    Identification: 0x76bc (30396)
  > Flags: 0x02 (Don't Fragment)
    Fragment offset: 0
    Time to live: 128
    Protocol: TCP (6)
    Header checksum: 0x0000 [validation disabled]
    [Header checksum status: Unverified]
    Source: 10.56.100.1
    Destination: 72.163.4.161
    [Source GeoIP: Unknown]
    [Destination GeoIP: Unknown]
```

The IP packet is depicted above. This is the OSI model's third layer. Don't worry about the different fields; we'll go over them later. At the top, the source and destination IP addresses are visible. Let us move on:

```
  4  Transmission Control Protocol, Src Port: 60522, Dst Port: 80, Seq: 1, Ack: 1, Len: 854
        Source Port: 60522
        Destination Port: 80
        [Stream index: 166]
        [TCP Segment Len: 854]
        Sequence number: 1    (relative sequence number)
        [Next sequence number: 855    (relative sequence number)]
        Acknowledgment number: 1    (relative ack number)
        Header Length: 20 bytes
      > Flags: 0x018 (PSH, ACK)
        Window size value: 64860
        [Calculated window size: 64860]
        [Window size scaling factor: -2 (no window scaling used)]
        Checksum: 0xbeed [unverified]
        [Checksum Status: Unverified]
        Urgent pointer: 0
      > [SEQ/ACK analysis]
```

The fourth layer of the OSI model is depicted above. The transport protocol in use here is TCP (which we will discuss later in detail). Last but not least, the final layer of the OSI model:

```
  7  Hypertext Transfer Protocol
      > GET / HTTP/1.1\r\n
        Host: cisco.com\r\n
        User-Agent: Mozilla/5.0 (Windows NT 10.0; WOW64; rv:49.0) Gecko/20100101 Firefox/49.0\r\n
        Accept: text/html,application/xhtml+xml,application/xml;q=0.9,*/*;q=0.8\r\n
        Accept-Language: nl,en-US;q=0.7,en;q=0.3\r\n
        Accept-Encoding: gzip, deflate\r\n
      > [truncated]Cookie: _ga=GA1.2.1395962453.1456492006; utag_main=v_id:01531db0e424001f457dae69
        Connection: keep-alive\r\n
        Upgrade-Insecure-Requests: 1\r\n
        \r\n
        [Full request URI: http://cisco.com/]
        [HTTP request 1/1]
        [Response in frame: 39687]
```

Layer seven, the application layer, is depicted above. There is no separate session or presentation layer visible here. This page contains more information about the HTTP protocol. We used a GET request to get to cisco.com, and the user agent I used was Mozilla (Firefox).

## Advantages of OSI Model

The OSI model assists computer network users and operators.

Determine the hardware and software needed to construct their network. Understand and communicate the process by which network components communicate with one another.

Troubleshoot by determining which network layer is causing the issue and focusing your efforts on that layer.

The OSI model assists network device manufacturers and networking software vendors:

Create devices and software that can communicate with any vendor's products, allowing for open interoperability.

Determine which network components their products should be compatible with.

Inform users about the network layers at which their product operates, such as whether it only operates at the application layer or across the stack.

## OSI vs. TCP/IP Model

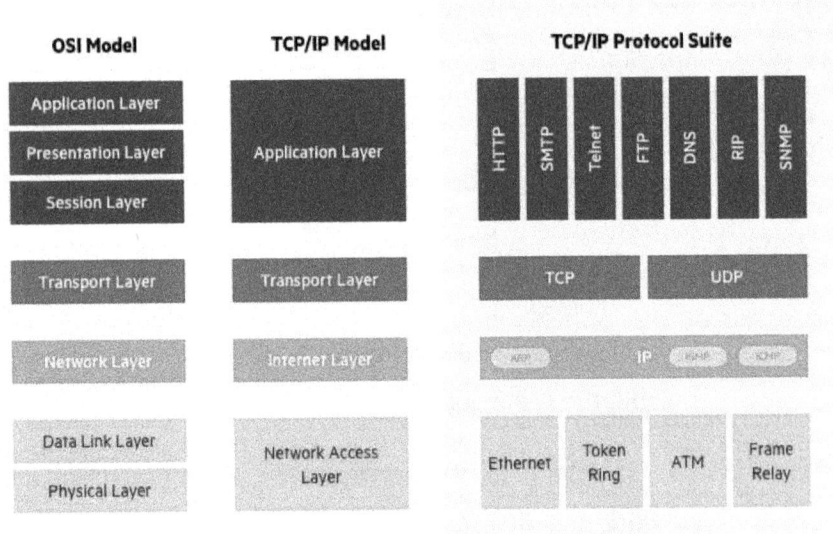

The OSI model predates the Transfer Control Protocol/Internet Protocol (TCP/IP) model, which was developed by the United States Department of Defense (DoD). TCP/IP is the more straightforward of the two models, combining multiple OSI layers into a single one,

TCP/IP combines OSI layers 5, 6, and 7 into a single Application Layer; however, TCP/IP does not handle sequencing or acknowledgment functions; these are handled by the underlying transport layer.

## Other important differences:

TCP/IP is a functional model that is built on specific, standard protocols to solve specific communication problems. OSI is a generic, protocol-independent model for describing all types of network communication.

Most TCP/IP applications employ all seven layers, whereas simple OSI applications do not. Data communication requires only layers 1, 2, and 3.

# References

1. Computer Networks by Andrew S. Tanenbaum
2. Data Communications and Networking by Behrouz A. Forouzan
3. TCP/IP Protocol Suite by Behrouz A. Forouzan
4. Internetworking with TCP/IP by Douglas E. Comer
5. Network Warrior by Gary A.
6. TCP/IP Illustrated by W. Richard Stevens
7. TCP/IP Guide by Charles M. Kozierok
8. TCP/IP Network Administration by Craig Hunt
9. Internetworking with TCP/IP by Douglas E. Comer
10. TCP/IP Sockets in C: Practical Guide for Programmers by Michael J. Donahoo and Kenneth L. Calvert

www.ingramcontent.com/pod-product-compliance
Lightning Source LLC
Chambersburg PA
CBHW061249040426
42444CB00010B/2320